THE STORY OF PRINCESS YENNENGA

By: Somanegre Lydie
K. Kafando

Illustrated by: Sara Khan

To Dad, for you are my idol.

To my children who inspire me.

A note from the author:

This story is not the original story.

I have read many princess stories to my children. I have always told them the story of Princess Yennenga. I decided to write a simplified and modified version to fit the environment that we live in.

“Tonight’s story is about an African Princess,” said Mom.

“I bet it is about Princess Yennenga,” said my brother. “Mom told us that story many times.”

“Mom, I want to hear about Princess Yennenga,” I said. “Please, please!”

“Mom has told us that story many times,” sighed my brother.

“Sure,” agreed Mom. “Settle in for the story.”

Long ago in Gambaga, West Africa, lived a King named King Nadéga. King Nadéga had many children. Yennenga, one of his children was intelligent, clever, brave, and beautiful. Her uncle, Sana, trained her, and she became one of King Nadéga's best warriors.

Uncle Sana was getting too old to lead the King's Army. He talked to the king about letting Yennenga lead the army. The king agreed.

Yennenga always returned victorious from the battlefield. She and her army kept the population safe and conquered many lands.

When Yennenga was not on the battlefield or with the army, she enjoyed gardening, making herself glamorous, and visiting her friends.

One day, while walking, King Nadéga saw that the okra from Yennenga's garden was getting old and drying out. The king was troubled that the Princess did not care for the okra. The king called the princess to ask her why. The princess was upset, too. She yelled at the king and was disrespectful to him. Then, the princess stomped away.

The king sent his guards to bring Princess Yennenga to the palace. She yelled at the king, "I don't have to listen to you. I am old enough to do what I want!" The king did not like Princess Yennenga's behavior, so he ordered the guard to lock the princess up.

One of the guards helped Princess Yennenga escape. She rode her horse toward the north of Gambaga.

Princess Yennenga rode for hours and hours through forests, winds, rain, and the desert. The brave princess even battled wild animals.

Fighting exhaustion, the princess fell asleep on her horse. The horse found a hut in the middle of the forest and stopped there. The hut belonged to a hunter named Rialé. Rialé heard the horse neighing. He went outside and saw Yennenga passed out on the horse. Rialé rescued Yennenga and cared for her.

As time went by, Yennenga and Rialé married and had a son. To honor the horse who brought Yennenga to Rialé, they named their son Ouédraogo, which means male horse.

Meanwhile, the King has been searching all horizons for his daughter. When he finally heard where she was, he sent his guards to return the princess and her family to her home.

Yennenga, her husband Rialé, and their son Ouédraogo returned to Gambaga. The king was thrilled to see his daughter again after many years. He was also delighted to meet his grandson. Yennenga apologized to the King for her behavior. The King forgave her and blessed her and her new family.

The king declared a three-day celebration for the return of his daughter and his grandson. The kingdom feasted, sang, and danced during those days. There were games, competitions, and shows.

Princess Yennenga and her family stayed for a month before returning. The king gave her an army, many horses, donkeys, cows, sheeps, goats, and farm goods. They traveled North of Gambaga and settled in a town called Tenkodogo to start their own kingdom.

Tenkodogo means old town and is considered the start of the Mossi kingdom, and Ouédraogo is considered the Mossi ancestor.

The end.

“Wow Mom! I loved the story!” I said.

“I am glad you did,” said Mom. “Good night, kids!”

“Good night,” said my brother.

“Good night, Mom!” Said my sister.

“Night-night, Mom!” I said as Mom kissed my forehead.

About the author:

Somanegre Lydie Karine Kafando was born in Burkina Faso. She has three children and lives in the United States of America. Somanegre enjoys sharing princess stories with her children. She also loves to sing and dance with her family.

www.ingramcontent.com/pod-product-compliance
Ingram Content Group UK Ltd.
Pitfield, Milton Keynes, MK11 3LW, UK
UKHW060119010826
14089UKWH00005B/56

9 798985 994322